Creative Careers

Interior Designer

Helen Mason

Gareth Stevens
PUBLISHING

Please visit our website, **www.garethstevens.com**. For a free color catalog of all our high-quality books, call toll free 1-800-542-2595 or fax 1-877-542-2596.

Library of Congress Cataloging-in-Publication Data

Mason, Helen.
Interior designer / by Helen Mason.
p. cm. — (Creative careers)
Includes index.
ISBN 978-1-4824-1336-6 (pbk.)
ISBN 978-1-4824-1291-8 (6-pack)
ISBN 978-1-4824-1447-9 (library binding)
1. Interior decoration — Vocational guidance — Juvenile literature. 2. Interior decoration—Juvenile literature.
I. Mason, Helen, 1950-. II. Title.
NK2116.M37 2015
729—d23

First Edition

Published in 2015 by
Gareth Stevens Publishing
111 East 14th Street, Suite 349
New York, NY 10003

Developed and produced for Gareth Stevens Publishing by BlueApple*Works* Inc.
Editor: Marcia Abramson
Art Director: Melissa McClellan
Designer: Joshua Avramson

Photo Credits: Corbis: © Pamela Hassell p. 40 bottom; Dreamstime: © Candybox Images title p.; © Stephen Coburn p. 8 top; © Irina88w p. 9 left; © Epstock p. 9 right; © Pavel Losevsky p. 12; © Brett Critchley p. 13; © Monkey Business Images p. 14 top; © Photographerlondon p. 16 top; © Krooogle p. 16; © Yaoyu Chen p. 17; © Piero Cruciatti p. 18; © Morphologics p. 19; © Mladen Bozickovic p. 26 top; © Sebastian Czapnik p. 26; © Lisa F. Young p. 32; © Dragonimages p. 33; © Imagecollect p. 41 top; © Sjankauskas p. 43; © Yuri_arcurs p. 44 top; J. Avramson p. 29; Public Domain: p. 7, 40 top; Shutterstock: © Tyler Olson cover; © Antoha713 cover top left; © Art'nLera cover top right; © Dropu bottom left; © Santiago Cornejo TOC background; © racorn TOC, p. 23 top, 28, 30 top; © Andresr p. 4; © jesadaphorn yellow note paper; © ollyy p. 5; © luchunyu p. 6; © gualtiero boffi p. 8; © Monkey Business Images p. 10 top, 23, 24, 36; © Pavel L Photo and Video p. 10; © Franck Boston p. 11; © Li Chaoshu p. 12 top, 45; © hxdbzxy p. 14; © Dmitry Kalinovsky p. 15 left; © vikiri p. 15 right; © liseykina p. 20 top; © GWImages p. 20 bottom; © Breadmaker p. 21 top; © David Hilcher p. 21; © Alexei Tacu p. 22 top; © bikeriderlondon p. 22; © Vladimir Gerasimov p. 25; © Goodluz p. 27; © aopsan p. 30; © CandyBox Images p. 31; © Layland Masuda p. 34; © Rob Marmion p. 34 bottom; © Dikiiy p. 35; michaeljung p. 37 left; © vvoe p. 37; © arek_malang p. 38; © wavebreakmedia p. 39; © Christopher Halloran p. 41; © Sean Pavone p. 42; © terekhov igor p. 44.

Manufactured in the United States of America

CPSIA compliance information: Batch #CS15GS. For further information contact Gareth Stevens, New York, New York at 1-800-542-2595.

Contents

What Is an Interior Designer?

Do you love color? Do you notice how it makes rooms feel different? Do you create different looks for your room, depending on how you feel? If you answered yes to any of these questions, then you might be happy with a career as an interior designer.

Interior refers to inside. Interior designers plan the way homes, businesses, and **institutions** look on the inside. They work with clients to get a feel for the client's needs and vision. The spaces they design look beautiful. They use colors to bring out the best in the furnishings and accessories.

Interior designers make sure the space fits the way it is used, whether as a morning exercise spot, a coffee drop-in, or an evening business meeting.

◄ An interior designer chooses the color palette for the space she is designing.

Qualities of a Designer

To be an interior designer, you need to develop many skills and talents. You must be creative and artistic, but you also must be practical. Interior design is a business, so you need to be organized and disciplined.

Interior designers need to have good communication skills. They must understand what clients want and then explain clearly how their designs will achieve the client's goals. Interior designers also must communicate well with **architects**, **contractors**, and other team members. They are the leader of the design project, but they need to be a team player as well.

▼ An interior designer discusses a newly-installed lighting system with the owner of this restaurant. The low lighting gives diners privacy.

Types of Interior Designers

Interior designers work on all kinds of projects, from houses to skyscrapers, but most focus on one type of design.

Ergonomic Designers

Ergonomics is the study of how to help people work without hurting themselves. To do this, interior designers study the work being done. Does it involve a lot of lifting? Do workers use computers? Do they meet often? This **analysis** is done by interviewing workers, observing them, and videotaping common tasks.

Ergonomic designers then plan spaces that are safer and more convenient. They place monitors at eye level and help workers find a chair that fits their body type and size. They redesign storage areas to reduce the amount of manual lifting and teach proper lifting techniques.

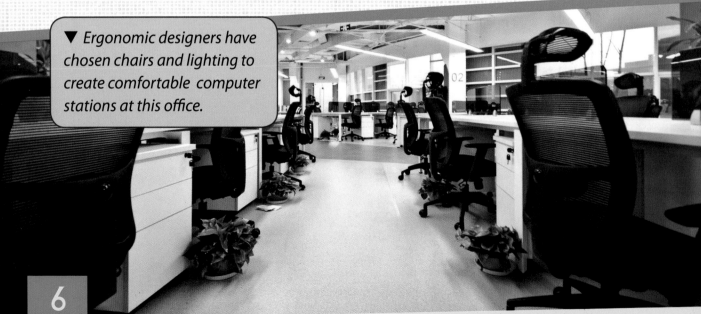

▼ *Ergonomic designers have chosen chairs and lighting to create comfortable computer stations at this office.*

Sustainable Designers

Sustainability refers to designs that are environmentally friendly. These designs reduce energy use, pollution, and waste. Sustainable designers use renewable materials from local sources. They recycle old materials and sometimes use products made from recycled ones. A new office building, for example, could be designed with carpeting made from recycled plastic bottles. A home bathroom could be remodeled with tiles made from recycled glass.

Large windows encourage the use of natural lighting. Triple-glazed windows with shutters or thermal curtains reduce heat loss. This saves energy.

Sustainable design is sometimes called "green design" because it aims to protect the planet.

▼ *Sustainable design was used inside and outside the California Academy of Sciences in San Francisco.*

Residential Designers

Residential designers design the interiors of houses, apartments, and **condos**.

New Construction

Whether the home is brand new or new to the client, an interior designer can make it more comfortable. This includes helping the client plan each space, providing information about design trends, and advising on materials for curtains and upholstery.

▲ *Interior designers plan rooms around personal collections and interests.*

Many designers start with a house tour. They study the **floor plan** and door and window placement. They notice when light enters the windows and how bright that light is. They listen to the client talk about personal interests. An interest in skiing or mountain biking might lead to a special area for sports equipment or trophies. Musicians might want speakers wired into the walls.

▼ *Organizers in this walk-in closet provide plenty of storage.*

Home Remodeling

Interior designers also work on renovations. Updating a bathroom is the most popular type of home renovation. Residential designers also remodel many kitchens with new counters, cabinets, and flooring. In older homes, the whole bathroom or kitchen may be gutted, or torn out. Then the designer creates a new, energy-efficient bathroom or kitchen.

If a client wants to enlarge the home, the designer's job gets much bigger!

▼ In bathroom renovations, designers often separate the shower from the bathtub.

▲ A former kitchen window has been enlarged to make a doorway to the patio.

9

Workplace Designers

Workplace designers plan new or redesigned office spaces.

Making the Space Work

Whether the office is small or large, a workplace designer aims to make it comfortable, efficient, and pleasant. The designer first considers how the space will be used. Should the office be open or have cubicles? How many computer stations must be created? Does the client need a reception area for visitors?

▲ *A designer goes through a workplace analysis with an employee.*

Once the basic layout is established, the designer selects carpeting, furniture, and even decorative plants and artwork.

▼ *This office was designed for news reporters and editors. The open design makes it easy for coworkers to communicate with each other.*

Finding the Right Spot

Businesses can buy, rent, or lease office space. Workplace designers study what is best for each business. Once a client decides what they want, designers research suitable properties. They analyze the advantages and disadvantages of each choice.

Technology is a special concern in selecting a site. Today's offices need electric power and outlets for multiple computers and other devices. New buildings are designed with this in mind, but an older office may need costly updating.

Did You Know?

Color can make a statement. The red, yellow, blue, and green colors from Google's logo are repeated in its office design. McDonald's red and yellow is used throughout its outlets.

▼ This interior designer has created a plan for turning this space into a lawyer's office.

Hospitality Designers

Hospitality designers plan restaurants, bars, clubs, hotels, and resorts.

Appealing to the Customers

Good interior design can make or break a business. The design must appeal to customers. To do this, designers study the market and develop a look that reflects the age and interests of customers.

▲ *The interior designer of this restaurant has created a sophisticated and elegant look.*

A family restaurant might have crayon-box colors with large tables and bright lighting. Romantic bars use subtle lighting and small tables for couples and intimate groups. The lighting in dance clubs often pulses with the music.

▼ *This nightclub has panels that change color with the music.*

Safety and Efficiency

A good hospitality design has attractive entrances with room for people to easily move in and out. The reception desk is large enough to hold menus and registration books. The area behind the desk should allow for free movement of employees. Movement is also important in the kitchen, where chefs move among food storage areas, cooking surfaces, and counters as they prepare and cook food.

Each place must meet local health and safety rules. This includes keeping walkways and exits clear. It also means planning enough electrical plugs so that extension cords are not needed.

▼ Hotel rooms must be designed to make the most of the small space. Many older hotels renovate their rooms to make them look more modern.

Healthcare Designers

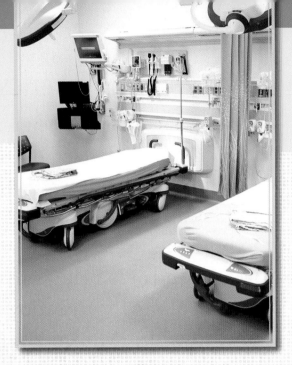

Healthcare designers work on doctors' offices, clinics, hospitals, and long-term care facilities.

User-Friendly

The people who use healthcare facilities include healthcare workers, patients, and visitors. Designers consider each of these groups. Plans must allow an efficient traffic flow for medical

▲ The floor in this hospital emergency room is made from jute. Jute is a natural material that resists bacteria.

workers, and patients must find the facility comfortable. Family members need places to wait, visit, or mourn.

Today, many hospitals and clinics focus on outpatient care. Patients come for treatment but do not stay overnight. These patients want a pleasant **atmosphere** that gives them privacy.

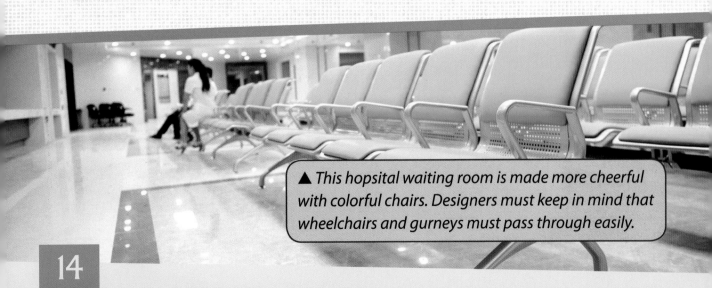

▲ This hopsital waiting room is made more cheerful with colorful chairs. Designers must keep in mind that wheelchairs and gurneys must pass through easily.

Safe and Sanitary

Hospitals and other healthcare facilities need a safe and sanitary environment. Design plans must include stations for hand washing and areas for disinfecting medical instruments, hospital gowns, and bed linens.

Good design can help prevent the spread of illness. The material of all furniture can be disinfected. Many hospitals hang hand sanitizers at all entrances. Sinks are clearly visible to someone entering a patient's room. This increases the chance of staff and visitors washing their hands before touching a patient.

▼ *Hospitals are busy places, so the halls need floors that are easy to clean.*

▲ *Healthcare designers put hand-sanitizing stations in locations that are easy to reach.*

Retail Designers

Retail, or store, designers work for stores that sell home furnishings.

In the Store

In-store designers work by appointment. In most cases, the service is free.

Designers help customers choose color schemes. They advise on the choice of paint, wallpaper, flooring, and counters, and may recommend lighting styles and suggest accessories.

Furniture store designers help put together the furnishings for a single room or an entire apartment. These designers get ideas from the furniture they have in stock. They also search through catalogues. Most are limited to the products carried by their store.

▼ *This bedroom features coordinating furniture and a pleasing color scheme.*

In the Home

For a fee, some stores offer at-home consultations. A designer visits the customer's home to get an idea of their space, tastes, and **budget**. At a follow-up appointment, she provides ideas. She shows fabric **swatches**, flooring samples, paint chips, and a selection of catalogues. Once the customer decides on what they want, she orders the necessary items. She has the items delivered and installed or set up.

▼ *Many furniture stores offer design services.*

Did You Know?

Some designers make accessory house calls. They visit a home and make notes about the decor. They later return with a truckload of accessories such as pillows, paintings, and figurines. Customers can pick what they want and return the rest.

▲ *Many stores have displays that show a complete room.*

Working for Yourself

Many designers work freelance. They charge by the hour, project, or square foot for the work they do.

Home or Away

Some freelancers have offices in their home. They use the design of their own home to display their talents. Others rent office space. The office is their work area and showroom.

It is important for freelancers to use their office space to show their flair for design. Many invest in the type of furnishings they recommend to clients. This can include becoming a **representative** for products they like.

Freelancers work long hours. Their job includes meeting with clients, doing site inspections, and attending opening parties to celebrate the completion of big jobs.

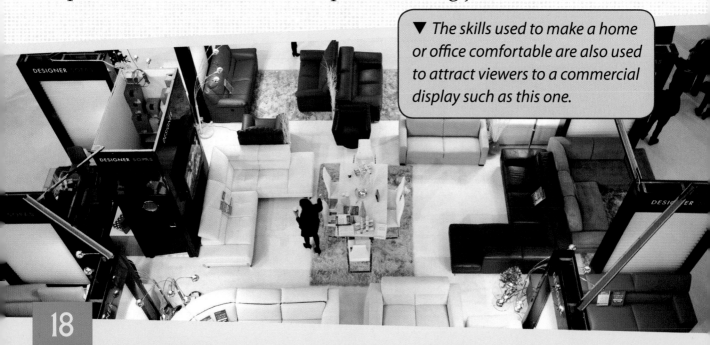

▼ *The skills used to make a home or office comfortable are also used to attract viewers to a commercial display such as this one.*

Special Skills

Many freelance designers specialize in business, residential, or healthcare work. They let the local market and their own interests decide.

Others focus on specific areas. Some designers plan the interiors of cottages, sailboats, and trailers. Others design displays for exhibitions and trade shows. Some may focus on sustainable design.

No matter what they specialize in, freelance designers must know how to run a business. They have to manage their own time and make sure that their deadlines are met. Often they are juggling more than one project at a time, but they need to keep all their clients happy.

Did You Know?

Interior designers make between $20,000 and $120,000 a year, depending on the number of hours they work and what they charge per hour. Their hourly rate takes into account their location, education, experience, and reputation, or branding.

◀ After specializing in home design, a designer may focus on a certain style such as minimalism, or very simple design.

19

Related Careers

Interior designers work with people in the following careers.

Interior Decorator

Interior decorators work for builders, businesses, and private clients. After consulting with a client, they provide decorating ideas. They measure and choose window treatments. They select artwork and accessories. They also coordinate the delivery of materials and may supervise crews doing hands-on work.

▲ *Decorators sometimes work on special events, such as weddings.*

Flooring Sales Representative

Flooring companies often have sales representatives. These reps sell to developers, contractors, and building owners. They sell carpet, tile, concrete, wood, and other finishes. They often visit the site with samples and to make recommendations.

◀ *This sales representative discusses floor finishes with a woman planning her first home.*

Kitchen and Bath Consultants

Kitchen and bath consultants help people plan renovations and updates. They explain the advantages and disadvantages of different finishes. They describe the latest trends. They help design a look that will work for clients.

▲ Some kitchen updates are as simple as changing the finish on cupboards and using new handles.

Feng Shui Consultant

Feng shui (pronounced fung shway) consists of placing objects so that energy flows freely around them. Feng shui consultants tour a house. Using the dates of birth of the people who live there, they suggest ways to organize furnishings in the most pleasing way. Feng shui is an Asian tradition.

▼ This living room includes pieces that represent fire, earth, water, metal, and wood.

The Work

Interior designers meet with clients, plan spaces for them, and then bring the plan to reality.

The First Meeting

The design process starts with a meeting with the client. A designer will ask: how will the space be used? How many people will use it? Are there any safety concerns? What colors and materials does the client like?

During this visit, the designer measures the space and studies the building. If walls are going to be removed, the designer wants to know whether they hold up the roof. Moving walls like that requires the help of an architect.

▲ *This model shows design suggestions for the work area in a large business.*

▶ *An interior designer and builder inspect condo units during construction. The designer will plan and design the entrance, halls, and recreation areas for the complex.*

Developing a Plan

After meeting with the client, the interior designer creates a plan for the space. The design ideas must suit the client's needs, space, and budget. Most designers present more than one option to the client.

They develop a color scheme and lighting for the space and suggest floor, window, and wall coverings. The plan also tells how long the project will take to complete and includes a budget that shows the cost of work and materials.

▲ This interior designer discusses fabric choices with a client.

▼ An interior designer and contractor go over plans for a space under construction with the clients.

The Design Process

Interior designers discuss their ideas with each client. They listen to the client's feedback. These changes are added to the drawings showing the plan.

The First Sketches

Once the client and designer have agreed on a basic plan, the designer creates preliminary sketches. These drawings give the look and feel of the design. They show a possible floor plan, a color scheme, and ideas for finishes. They also suggest a price.

▼ *The designer and client study the sketches together and discuss changes.*

24

The Final Plan

Once the design is final, the designer makes detailed drawings for each part of the design. The client then must approve the final design. Now the designer begins working with contractors to create the space. This part includes choosing flooring, finding the right fabric for window coverings, and selecting furniture.

Designers keep an eye on the job while it's being done. Did the correct materials come in? Are they being put in properly? What building codes must be followed? Are there any health and safety issues that need to be resolved?

▼ This bathroom sketch includes a bathtub, shower, and shelving.

The Production Process

Using the final design and detailed drawings, the interior designer creates the space.

Managing the Project

The designer shares his detailed drawings with contractors and any architect needed for the job. He checks safety regulations and applies for permits. He also plans a project timeline.

▲ *This design includes exposing the brick wall. The designer checks with an architect to make sure the plan is safe.*

Contractors provide estimates for their part of the job. The designer reviews these and may make suggestions to the client. Some designers hire the contractors, too.

The designer orders everything needed. He wants it all ready before work starts. During construction, he oversees the work. He keeps an eye on the schedule and meets with the client to discuss progress.

▼ *The interior designer designs the paint scheme, but hires contractors to do the actual painting.*

Finishing Touches

The flooring is down. The paint is on. The furniture is in. Now the interior designer sees how everything has come together and makes final adjustments. Did the painters miss a spot? Has the carpet been laid smoothly? Has everything been cleaned up properly?

When the designer is satisfied, he presents the space to the client—who often reacts with lots of "oohs" and "aahs." Clients are happy to see their vision become reality, and the designer is happy to have done a good job.

▶ As the designer and client tour this finished home, the designer lists items that still need attention.

Tools and Skills

Interior designers use drawing and measuring tools, color palettes, and material swatches.

High-Tech Designs

Technology simplifies interior design work. Digital cameras record the original condition of each space and show the progress. Photos are used to communicate with clients and to advertise successful work.

Designers use smartphones to take notes during client meetings. Various apps allow them to transfer this information to their desktop computer or iPad. They can also track their time and make schedules.

Most interior designs use computer-aided design (**CAD**). Using more than one computer monitor gives them more flexibility. They can design on one monitor and track costs on another. Interior designers use color palette generators to help with color selection for their projects.

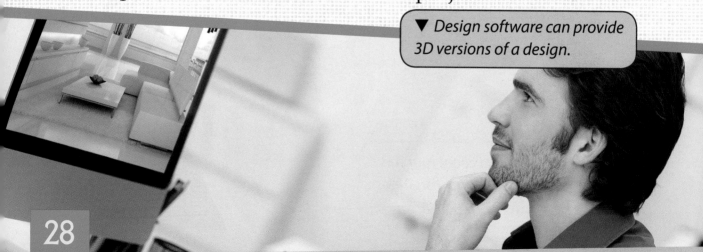

▼ *Design software can provide 3D versions of a design.*

Gathering Samples

Sample boards are used to show clients how the elements of a design will come together. A typical sample board includes a layout of the design, fabric swatches, and paint chips to show the proposed colors. If wood, carpet, wallpaper, or tile is being used, those samples are on the board, too.

The designer and client study the sample board and make choices together. Often they do this in the space being designed, so they can see how the samples look there.

Did You Know?

Sitting facing a door suggests power and authority. An award-winning office design shows desks with the computers facing a front corner. From that angle, workers can see anyone walking by. They feel safe.

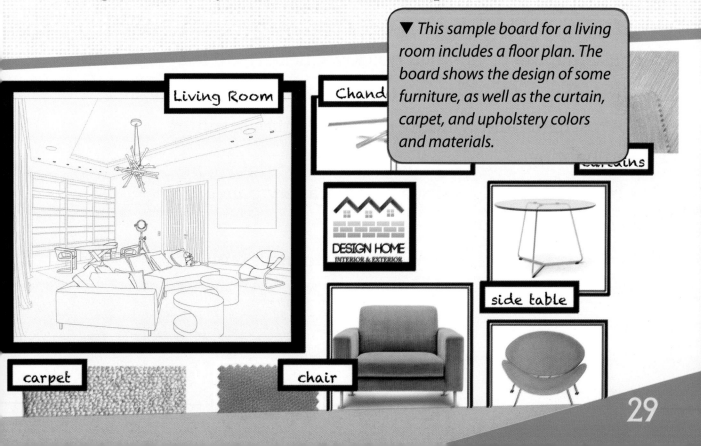

▼ *This sample board for a living room includes a floor plan. The board shows the design of some furniture, as well as the curtain, carpet, and upholstery colors and materials.*

Living Room

Chand

DESIGN HOME
INTERIOR & EXTERIOR

curtains

side table

carpet

chair

A Day in the Life of an Interior Designer

An interior designer keeps busy in and out of the office. A typical day can include meetings with contractors and clients, studying design trends, and even putting up curtains!

Here's a sample schedule.

Morning

▲ *A lot of the day is spent meeting with clients, listening to their needs, and making recommendations.*

9:00 a.m. — Arrive at office. Go online to check the latest design news.

9:15 a.m. — Check email. Deal with urgent messages and those that can be handled quickly. Check to-do list.

10:00 a.m. — Greet client. Review rec room plan. Choose color scheme and window fabrics. Discuss furniture and lighting.

10:30 a.m. — Say goodbye. Load drapery panels and hardware into van.

11:30 a.m. — Eat lunch on the way to meet with another client.

Afternoon

12:10 p.m. — Meet drapery installer at client's. Check measurements and put up drapes.

3:30 p.m. — Make sure client is happy. Admire drapes together.

3:45 p.m. — Head for new apartment complex.

4:00 p.m. — Meet with builder. Measure the rooms for a model unit. Discuss some ideas.

5:15 p.m. — Back in office. Add model plan to to-do list. Place some online orders. Check social media.

6:15 p.m. — Check email. Answer some of the more time-consuming messages from the morning.

6:45 p.m. — Recheck to-do list. Send congratulatory letter to a client who just opened a restaurant.

Did You Know?

The wood graining you see in many expensive homes is painted by hand. Designers use combs, brushes, stencils, and other tools to make wood look as though it has knots and rich grain. This skill dates back to ancient Egypt.

Becoming an Interior Designer

Interior design is a great profession that makes a real difference in people's lives. Designers create spaces that look good and function well for families and businesses. You'll work hard, but get great satisfaction. Here are some ways to get started.

Start at Home

○ If your parents will let you, paint your room. Research different colors. Choose one that makes a statement. Don't worry about getting a look you dislike. You can always repaint!

○ Help family and friends with their decorating. This can include painting, hanging wallpaper, and putting up curtains.

○ Train your eye to pick up details. Decide what you like and dislike about various spaces. How would you improve them?

○ Flip through design magazines and check out online sites looking for designs.

▼ *Your parents can show you how to paint walls.*

Visit and Join

Touring model homes is a great way to learn about design. These homes are move-in ready down to the last detail. You can also see model rooms at some furniture stores.

Joining a camera club is another good idea for future designers. Taking pictures is often part of the job!

Finally, if your family knows an interior designer, volunteer to run errands or help in the office. This is a great way to start learning.

▼ You can go to your local library to pick up ideas from design magazines and books.

Education

Interior designers finish high school. They then go to a university or community college.

High School

Many high school courses teach skills needed for interior design.

▲ *High school art classes teach sketching skills.*

- Art classes give experience with sketching tools and practice using color for different effects.
- English classes teach communication skills.
- Math classes provide a background in measuring.
- Computer classes provide experience with different software programs and applications.
- Home economics classes deal with fabrics.
- Drafting and construction classes provide training in floor plans.

▲ *Home economics provides useful experience with colors, fabrics, and design.*

After High School

Most interior designers have a degree or certificate in interior design. Some have studied 3D design, graphic design, fashion and textile design, architecture, or fine art.

After training, they get experience, often as assistants or **apprentices**. During this time, they work with certified interior designers. They improve their listening skills and may start to manage work crews. Some take courses in upholstery, decorating techniques, feng shui, or CAD.

Designers keep up to date with trends and new products. After several years of work, they take a certification exam. In some states, they also need to be licensed.

▼ This university student prepares a sample design.

35

Internship Programs

When they finish school, new interior designers work with an experienced designer for one to three years.

What an Intern Does

Interior designers must get experience in the field before they can be certified. Internships allow this. During an internship, interns work for a design company or store with design services.

An intern may start by taking care of the sample libraries. They create job binders to keep track of projects and maintain lists of workers on each project. They put together and arrange furniture for model units. They also order and sometimes pick out furniture.

As they get more experience, they draft floor plans, develop budgets, and check building codes. They need to practice everything they learned in school.

◀ *Mentors* help interns understand the variety of opportunities in interior design.

Interior Design Experience Program

The Interior Design Experience Program (IDEP) is run by the National Council for Interior Design Qualification. During this program, interns work, observe, and get additional training.

They start by finding a business willing to hire them. There, they work with a **supervisor** or employer who keeps an eye on their progress. Several times a year, they meet with a mentor who encourages them. At the end of their program, interns are ready to take the certification exam.

Did You Know?

Are you interested in becoming an intern when you are older? Opportunities are available both in the United States and abroad. Check for opportunities by googling "interior design internships" and following the links.

▼ *Interns who work abroad learn about the building styles and design ideas in other cultures.*

Design Portfolio

A portfolio is a collection of sketches and photos of a designer's work. Designers use portfolios to show what they can do.

Create Your Own

Once you start designing, you can make your own design portfolio to show off your best work.

Use a leather binder, photo album, or good quality portfolio. Look for one that allows you to change the order and number of pages.

Start by introducing yourself, your background, and your work. What motivates you? What do you want to do with your designs?

Insert floor plans, pictures of sample boards, sketches, and photos of your best projects. Briefly describe them, if they need it.

Try to show the design process for a number of projects. Keep each one brief.

Include CAD work if you have some. It will separate you from other candidates when you apply for programs and internships.

Getting a Job

Along with portfolios, new interior designers include a resume when they apply for a job. A resume lists all your education and any kind of experience that relates to the job. It's important to make sure everything is spelled right on your resume!

Interior designers use their creative skills in their portfolios and resumes. This gives employers an idea of what they can do.

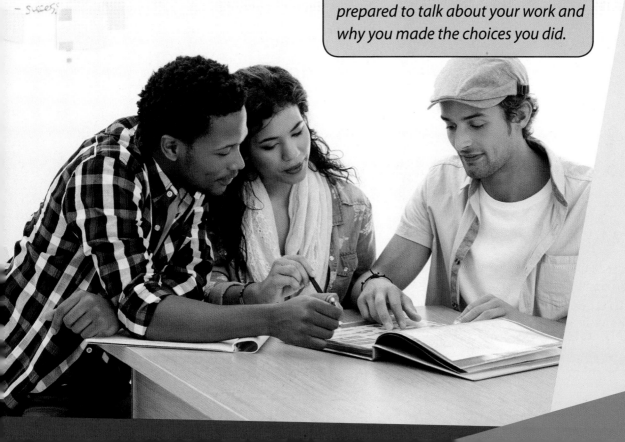

▼ When showing your portfolio, be prepared to talk about your work and why you made the choices you did.

Learning from the Masters

Dorothy Draper

In 1939, Dorothy Draper (1889–1969) wrote *Decorating Is Fun!* That book helped to start America's home improvement trend. She decorated many of America's top hotels. Her work is so well-respected that the Museum of the City of New York had a special display.

▲ *Dorothy Draper learned about interior decor by visiting expensive homes in the United States and Europe.*

Rose Tarlow

Born in Shanghai, China, in 1946, Rose Tarlow works in Los Angeles, where her rooms are considered lessons in design and in living. Tarlow designs furniture, textiles, wallpaper, and leathers. Her 2001 book, *The Private House*, advises people to arrange their large pieces of comfortable furniture first.

◄ *Rose Tarlow also has a furniture line of look-alike antiques.*

Vern Yip

Born in Hong Kong in 1968, Vern Yip is based in Atlanta, Georgia. This designer and TV personality is well-known for creating spaces where people can live and connect with their family and friends. He suggests that people reduce their possessions and display the things that mean a lot to them.

▲ Vern Yip suggests that people's rooms should show what they love.

Nate Berkus

Born in Orange County, California in 1971, he runs his own design firm Nate Berkus Associates. He was a regular guest on *The Oprah Winfrey Show*, offering design advice to viewers. He has written two books, *Home Rules: Transform the Place You Live Into a Place You'll Love*, and *The Things That Matter*.

▶ Nate Berkus has designed a new product line for Target.

How Interior Design Evolved

Although people have been decorating since the early humans painted on cave walls, the profession of interior designer is just over 100 years old. What began with simple function, taste, and style has become a booming industry filled with talented designers who transform spaces.

Early Design

In America, the term "interior decorator" wasn't used until after 1900, and it wasn't until 1913 that an interior decorator was paid for her work. Elsie de Wolfe, the first professional decorator, is the woman who paved the way for modern designers.

Department stores also appeared in the early 1900s. These stores designed rooms to help sell their furniture. Some stores started offering design services.

In the 1930s, interior decorators started being referred to as interior designers. This shift in terminology was the result of design magazines at the time.

▼ *This early department store was the first department store of its kind in Philadelphia.*

20th Century and Beyond

In 1931, a group of decorators started the American Institute of Decorators. This was changed to the American Institute of Interior Designers in 1936. The US National Society of Interior Designers was established in 1957.

To be marketable in today's competitive market, interior designers must understand all aspects of design and function while specializing in certain areas.

In the early years of interior decorating, a formal education was not required, but today, a career as an interior designer requires years of study as well as experience.

▼ Stores still sell furniture by presenting entire rooms for customers to replicate.

You Can Be an Interior Designer

Do you still want to be an interior designer? Check out the following characteristics. Which traits do you have? Which ones are you developing?

▲ *Help friends and family with their interior decorating.*

I am
- ❐ interested in design
- ❐ artistic
- ❐ good with budgets
- ❐ organized
- ❐ hardworking

I enjoy
- ❐ creating spaces that people enjoy
- ❐ working with color and texture
- ❐ listening to people's needs and ideas

If you have or are developing these traits, you might make a great interior designer.

▼ *Study old furniture. Good design is timeless. What worked in the past can be adapted for today's rooms.*

Set Your Goal

Decide where you want to study interior design. Research the needed training either online or by talking to a guidance counselor. You will want to find out:

- What high school credits do you need?
- What other experience would be useful?
- What schools offer the courses you want?
- What grades do you need to get into those schools?

▲ *When you take a vacation, you can get design ideas from the places you visit.*

Take Steps Now

Offer to help design and build sets for student or amateur theater. This work will teach you how to create atmosphere using a small amount of furniture and accessories.

Make a dollhouse and decorate it to reflect the interests of a sibling or young friend.

Make notes about the sets and rooms you create. Draw each floor plan. Sketch the original idea. Photograph the results.

Post samples of your work online. Subscribe to the blogs of well-known designers. Learn what people like about their work and then develop a style of your own.

Glossary

accessible able to be reached or understood

analysis a study of something to discover its parts and how they fit together

apprentice a person who learns a job or skill by working for a fixed period of time for a professional in a certain field

architect a person who designs buildings and supervises construction

atmosphere the main mood or feeling in a place or a work of art, such as a movie

budget a plan for using money, or the amount of money available for a specific purpose

CAD abbreviation for computer-aided design, or using special computer software for precision drawing

color palette a set of colors being used for a project

condo an individually-owned dwelling that is part of a larger building or group of buildings

contractor a person who agrees to do work or provide supplies at a certain price and often within a certain time

floor plan a detailed drawing that shows a room as seen from above

institution an established organization or corporation

mentor a wise adviser or teacher

mosaic a decoration that uses small pieces of glass, tile, or stone to make pictures or patterns

neutral a word to describe something plain that does not stand out; colors that are not bright or bold

renovation the process of making something new again, or remodeling it

representative someone who acts on behalf of another person

supervisor a person in charge who directs the work of others

swatch a small piece used as a sample, usually of fabric

For More Information

Books

Smith, Lucy. *Love Your Home: A Beginner's Guide to Interior Design.* London: Endeavour Press Ltd., 2012.

Weaver, Janice. *It's Your Room: A Decorating Guide for Real Kids* Toronto: Tundra Books, 2006.

Websites

American Society of Interior Designers
www.asid.org
Learn about a career in interior design.

Home Designing
www.home-designing.com/category/teen-room-designs
Experiment with some of these ideas in your own room.

Interior Design
www.interiordesign.net
Keep up to date on the latest trends and styles.

National Council for Interior Design Qualification
www.ncidq.org/idep.aspx
Interior Design Experience Program (IDEP)

Publisher's note to educators and parents: Our editors have carefully reviewed these websites to ensure that they are suitable for students. Many websites change frequently, however, and we cannot guarantee that a site's future contents will continue to meet our high standards of quality and educational value. Be advised that students should be closely supervised whenever they access the Internet.

Index